IMAGES
of America

GIBRALTAR

This 1950 aerial view of Gibraltar includes the mainland (top) and, from left to right, Edmund Island, Hall Island, and Horse Island. Because of its position on the waterfront, Gibraltar can be completely cut off from its neighbors by simply closing the three Gibraltar Roads. Edmund Hall, who owned most of the property in the mid-1800s, started dredging along the riverfront and Horse Island. In the 1920s, dredging continued around the other islands and bridges were completed.

ON THE COVER: The old Gibraltar School and Church is seen in November 1938 after the first snowfall. Otto Townsend's horse and sleigh are in the front. Teachers Cleo Parsons and Norma Shrader are in the back row on the right. Their students are, in no particular order, Ross Denison, Joyce Denison, Rita Denison, Dale Underwood, Shirley Underwood, Elaine Blakely, Robert Hoeft, Eugene Gadille, Donald Gadille, Earl Shuknecht, Shirley Shuknecht, Gerald Peer, Gloria Peer, Joan Munro, Mary Munro, Edgar Forcier, Helen Forcier, Louise Pavalock, Eta Langlois, Joe Glidden, Barbara Burt, Dwight Burt, Lorraine Freda, Lorraine Richie, Mary Lou Vance, Wallace Townsend, Doris Townsend, Elizabeth Rogers, Russell Smith, Rita Dillon, Maxine Chastain, Robert Dailey, Alfred Frank, Laura Frank, Donald (Zee) Harrison, James Demare, Conrad Walters, Bruce Steffke, James Knight, Robert Peshke, Marilyn Bidelman, Norma Rick, Martha Watt, Vincent Rahn, Edward Williams, John Laub, William Fickle, Catherine Rahn, Robert Daily, Donna Hershey, Marilyn Scholl, Donald Bowen, Enid Cook, Grace Smith, and Paul Batten.

IMAGES
of America

GIBRALTAR

Dorothy Wood for the
Gibraltar Historical Museum

ARCADIA
PUBLISHING

Published by Arcadia Publishing
Charleston, South Carolina

Library of Congress Control Number: 2013934397

For all general information, please contact Arcadia Publishing:
Telephone 843-853-2070
Fax 843-853-0044
E-mail sales@arcadiapublishing.com
For customer service and orders:
Toll-Free 1-888-313-2665

Visit us on the Internet at www.arcadiapublishing.com

*This book is dedicated to everyone fascinated
in preserving the history of Gibraltar.*

CONTENTS

ACKNOWLEDGMENTS

I would like to thank the following persons who provided images and histories of Gibraltar and its families, without which this book would not have been possible: the Hedke family, Bonnie Dougherty, Joann Kline, Don Comella, Julie Storm, Jim Canterbury, Norman Gerow, William Heinrich, Robert Wright, and the International Wildlife Refuge. I would like to give a big thank-you and much appreciation to my husband, John, for his continued support of all of my volunteer efforts. And a very special thank-you goes to Fay (Blakely) Steelman for preserving detailed records of her family's history. The Blakely story also includes the Munros, Parsons, and Denisons. I am grateful to Ross Denison for family images and delightful stories about Gibraltar's past.

Fred Wall and his wife, Sandy (Dahlka), shared their family histories and images. I am told that, if you need to know anything about Gibraltar, just ask Fred. I wish to thank Warren Heier Jr. for the images and information he provided about the Hall farm, which his family once owned, as well as his help with proofreading and corrections concerning Gibraltar details. Clive Taylor provided images about Gibraltar, duck hunting, and Pointe Mouillee. Frank and Janet Bevins shared images and information about their home, which was Gibraltar's second lighthouse. I thank Linda Bromund for all of her Gibraltar knowledge and the photographs of her father's business, Champ's Gas Station. And I cannot leave out Doris Bobier and Nancy Benyo for writing *Gibraltar: Our Story, 1776–1976* for the bicentennial. Their extensive and painstaking research proved to be a valuable resource in the writing of this book. Except where noted, images are from the city of Gibraltar archives.

INTRODUCTION

Before Gibraltar was platted, it was home to the Wyandot (also known as Huron) tribe of Native Americans and the location of the Wyandot council fire. In one of the earliest maps of this area, dated 1749, the French refer to it as Chenal de la Presque Isle. The French also called this area Grosse Roche, meaning "big rock."

Villages settled in the late 1700s in close proximity to Gibraltar were Brown's Town, named after Adam Brown, and Walker's. The Battle of Brownstown during the War of 1812 was fought at Brownstown Creek and River Road, where Oscar A. Carlson High School is today. After the war, one of the first early settlers to Gibraltar was Cornelius Springstead in 1818. Other early settlers to this area were the Blakelys, arriving in 1836. The Munro and Parsons families were also some of the first settlers. Because of the fertile land and heavily wooded area along the Detroit River, settlers came here to farm, and lumbermen and shipbuilders made this their home.

Gibraltar, in Wayne County, was platted and recorded on March 14, 1837, by Peter Godfroy, Benjamin B. Kercheval, and Joshua Howard. They were trustees of the Gibraltar and Flat Rock Land and Canal Company, which had plans to build a canal across the state, from Gibraltar to Muskegon, to connect the Detroit River with Lake Michigan. Their plans brought more settlers to the area. However, the project failed. On the 1837 plat of Gibraltar, at the end of Coral Street and on the edge of the Detroit River, was noted "Big Rock." Over the years, as the shoreline eroded, the rock became submerged. Since the rock is now covered by water and muck, it has been seen only when the water level is extremely low.

Shipbuilding at the Linn and Craig shipyard was going strong at this time, and the first lighthouse was constructed in 1837. There were a few small general stores, a post office, and homes of ship- and boatbuilders in Gibraltar proper from 1854 to 1899. The homes and businesses were located along the banks of the Detroit River, from Middle Gibraltar Road to Grandview Street, and toward the river where Lowell Street is today. Edmund Hall, a lawyer and wealthy businessman, owned much of the area past Grandview Street that included Horse Island. He had a large farm with cattle, but only used it during the summers. The rest of the year, he paid people $1 per day to work there. River Road, the main thoroughfare at that time, was always muddy. It would take farmers a full day to reach Detroit with the produce they were taking to market.

After shipbuilding left in the late 1800s, Gibraltar was a very poor area. Life was slow and simple. The people tried to be self-sufficient by hunting and fishing, and everyone had a garden.

During Prohibition, in the early 1920s, a surprising amount of people living in Gibraltar participated in bootlegging or rum-running. Times were not good, and people needed to do what they could to support their families. It was a dangerous game, and one needed to know one's way around the marshes. During the winter, when the river froze over, bootleggers would drive their cars across the river to Canada. They drove with their door open in case the car went through the ice.

After Prohibition, prominent families from Detroit claimed this area for summer homes and cottages. During the Depression, people started to live here year-round. They could no longer afford their main home in the city and also a summer home. In the 1920s, there were roughly 20 permanent homes here.

McLouth Steel Corporation built a stainless steel mill here in 1954. In fact, McLouth owned more land in Gibraltar than did the city at that time. Because of the taxes that the firm paid, the area thrived. Gibraltar was incorporated as a village in 1954; Hy Dahlka was the first village president. Workers were moving into town, and throughout the late 1950s and 1960s, homes, churches, and schools were built. Between 1960 and 1969, 436 homes went up. There was a municipal building, police and fire station, and department of public works. Gibraltar had everything it needed to take care of its own. Besides a grocery store, drug store, post office, hair salon, barber shop, gas station, dentist, and doctor, there were a few small businesses and marinas, along with a pizzeria and a Dairy Queen. The small town had a population of 2,187 when it became a city in 1961. Charles Shumate was the city's first mayor, serving until 1971.

One

HUMBLE BEGINNINGS

This map shows Gibraltar as it was from 1750 to 1812. Gibraltar is the area in the upper right corner, to the right of Brown's Town and below Walkers. It is a small, marshy area on the banks of the Detroit River, midway between Detroit and Toledo. The Wyandots of the Turtle band lived in the surrounding area.

BATTLE OF

BROWNSTOWN

1 In this vicinity on Aug. 5, 1812, six
2 weeks after the outbreak of war,
3 about 25 Indians, led by the famous
4 Shawnee chief, Tecumseh, ambushed
5 a 200-man American force under Maj.
6 Thomas Van Horne which was on its
7 way south to the River Raisin. There,
8 supplies vitally needed by Hull's army
9 in Detroit were awaiting an escort
10 through the Indian blockade of the
11 River Road. Tecumseh opened fire as
12 the Americans forded Brownstown
13 Creek. Van Horne, overestimating the
14 Indians' numbers, ordered his men to
15 fall back. The retreat soon became
16 a panic-stricken flight back to Fort
17 Detroit. Seventeen Americans were
18 killed, 12 wounded, and two captured
19 and murdered. One Indian was killed.

Michigan Historical Commission Registered Site No. 100

The Battle of Brownstown, in 1812, was fought along Brownstown Creek and River Road, which is now West Jefferson. The Oscar A. Carlson High School stands on the site today. Shown here is the inscription describing the battle that was engraved on the plaque. The plaque has been moved from Parsons Elementary School to its new location on South Gibraltar Road.

In the 1890s, Dr. H.C. Wyman purchased the land at the site of the battle, built his summer home nearby, and, in 1902, began to erect a memorial. He died in the spring of 1908 and never saw the dedication of the monument, which took place in August 1908. In 1957, road-widening forced the monument to be moved to its location on Middle Gibraltar Road near Parsons Elementary School. Shown here are, from left to right, Rocky Rokicak, Dwight Burt, Bob Detlor, Frank Gilbo, Dwight Smith, Tom Detlor, and Arnold Kuster. Wayne County employees are in the truck in the background.

The monument cannons are pictured being moved into place. Looking on are, from left to right, two unidentified Wayne County employees, Arnold Kuster, Adele Rahn, and Frank Gilbo. Rahn was Gibraltar's historian in the 1950s.

Shown here is the completed memorial of the Battle of Brownstown, including the plaque, cannons, and the Earl Wood log cabin. The memorial stands in front of Cleo Parsons Elementary School. When more room was needed for parking at the school, the memorial needed to be moved. The cannons and plaque are now on South Gibraltar Road, and only pieces of the log cabin remain in the Gibraltar Historical Museum.

The Earl Wood log cabin, originally on River Road, was later moved to Middle Gibraltar Road. John Wood was born in Dumphries, Scotland, on March 4, 1820. In April 1840, he purchased a farm in the Township of Brownstown, now the southern part of Gibraltar. One of John and Sarah Wood's sons, Luther Wood, married Frances Stoflet. Their son Earl was born in this log cabin. Below, on October 5, 1958, the cabin was again dedicated, along with a Michigan historical marker. In 1961, this was the oldest log cabin in Michigan.

This map was copied from the *Illustrated Atlas of Wayne County 1876.* In the center, closest to the Detroit River, are the Gibraltar claims. Among the claims shown are those of James Blakely (son of Hiram Blakely, who originally owned the land), the Alanson Parson family, and Edmund Hall. Gibraltar proper is the grid between the Hall properties on the Detroit River.

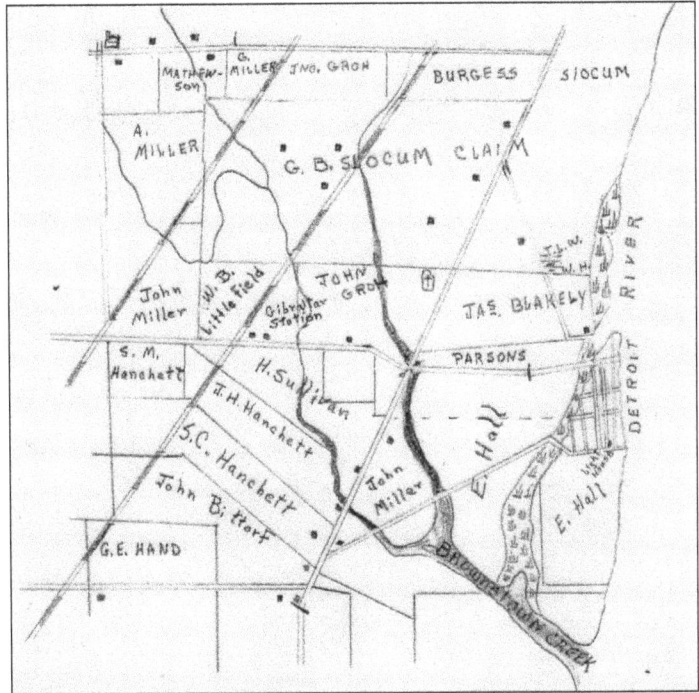

Hiram Blakely was born on May 11, 1803. He and his wife, Eliza, and their family came to Gibraltar in 1836 from Saratoga Springs, New York. Their home was located on Blakely Street and North Gibraltar Road. Members of the Hiram Blakely family are seen here standing outside their home in the 1800s. Grandmother Phebe Blakely is pictured on the left. (Courtesy Fay Blakely Steelman.)

Phebe Blakely was born in 1776 and died 92 years later, on July 12, 1868. Her son Hiram died on May 26, 1865. Both are buried in the Gibraltar Cemetery. (Courtesy Fay Blakely Steelman.)

Hiram D. Blakely, also known as Dee, is seen traveling to market. He recalled often going to Detroit with his father, James, taking a load of farm produce to market. He would point out the Truax House on River Road, saying, "that's the first place my grandparents stayed when they came to Michigan." (Courtesy Fay Blakely Steelman.)

Farming and shipbuilding were the major forms of livelihood in the 1800s. Hiram D. Blakely (September 14, 1865–October 8, 1940) is seen in these photographs working the field with his team of horses, Maude and Bud. He owned one of the few dairy farms in the area. The others were owned by Ostreich and Charlie Groves. The Blakelys also ran the Blakely Tavern, which housed most of the area's shipbuilders. The tavern was located on Davis and Washington (now Lowell) Streets. Hiram was the postmaster from 1845 to 1856. (Courtesy Fay Blakely Steelman.)

In the late 1800s, farmers possessing mechanical equipment, such as these tractors and threshing machines, would travel from farm to farm in the spring, helping farmers get their land ready for planting crops. In addition to these machines, farmers would bring their own tools and animals to work the land. It is unclear if these services were paid for in money or through a barter system. (Courtesy Ross Denison.)

Wayne Co. Farmers'
INSTITUTE

STEPHEN PEARL, President,................Belleville, Mich.
JAMES C. PULLEN, Secretary,................Belleville, Mich.

School House, Gibraltar, Mich.,

MONDAY, FEBRUARY 21st, 1916.

COUNTY ROUND-UP, AT REDFORD. FEB. 23-24, 1916.

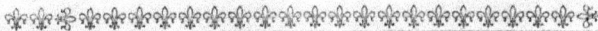

PROGRAM

E. L. DENISON, Vice President.

Morning 9:30 o'clock

Introductory remarks by Mr. Pearl, President Co. Farmers' Institute.

Music

"Alfalfa and Other Legumes"—
    State Speaker, Chas. B. Scully, of Almont

Discussion.

Music.

Dinner Served by the Grange—25c.

Afternoon 1:00 o'clock.

Music.

"Better Live Stock, Why and How"—State Speaker, Chas. B. Scully

Poultry Topic—Mrs. Wagar.

Question Box.

Music.

Supper Served by the Grange—25c.

Evening 7:15 o'clock.

Music.

"The Life Worth While"—State Speaker, Charles B. Scully.

Recitation.

"School Subject"—H. R. Pattengill, of Lansing.

Music.

This flyer announces the Wayne County Farmers' Institute meeting. It was held on Monday, February 21, 1916, at the Gibraltar School. Edmund L. Denison was vice president of the institute at that time.

Nellie Blakely, the granddaughter of James Blakely, married Edmund Denison, and they built their home and farm (pictured here) on their portion of the original Blakely farm. Their only son, Bryce, also built his home on their property. Bryce married Emma Bishop, and they had seven children—six daughters and one son. Their son, Ross Denison, also built his home on the property of the original Blakely farm. (Courtesy Ross Denison.)

James Blakely married Anna Dunivan in 1863. Posing for this photograph in the early 1930s are members of the Blakely and Dunivan families with their children. They are gathered at Edmund and Nellie Denison's home. (Courtesy Fay Blakely Steelman.)

Looking south, this view shows the Denison farm in the early 1930s. The home and barn are on the right side of North Gibraltar Road. The area on the left is where Humbug Too, part of the Humbug Marina, is today. (Courtesy of Ross Denison.)

In this view of the Denison farm, looking north on North Gibraltar Road, the home and barn are on the left. The sheep pasture, on the left, is today the site of the International Wildlife Refuge. (Courtesy of Ross Denison.)

The Gibraltar and Flat Rock Land and Canal Company was organized on July 20, 1836, with the ultimate goal of constructing a connecting waterway from Gibraltar to Muskegon to economically transport passengers and freight. Leaders associated with the project were Lewis Cass and Daniel Webster. The company's offers of work filled the area with new settlers. Michael Beaulieu is shown here in 1961, standing in part of the canal that was started on the south side of Gibraltar Road. Traces of the early stages of the canal can still be seen today.

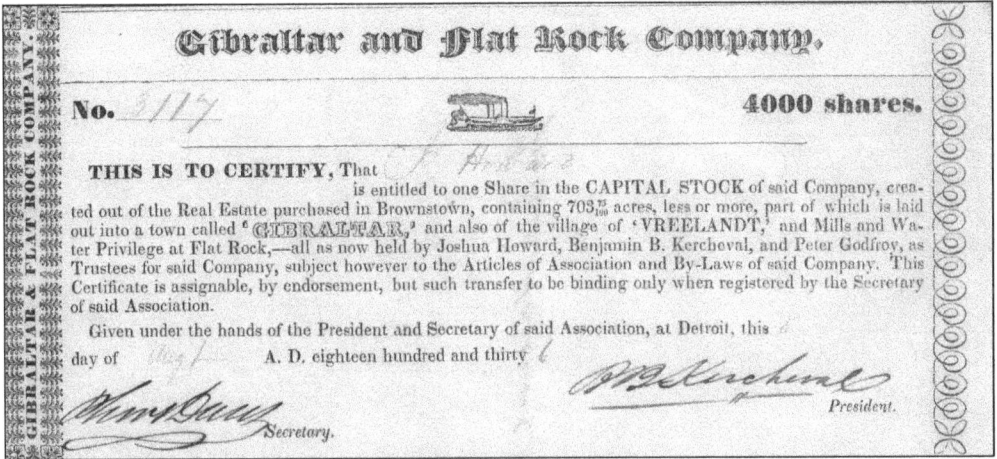

Gibraltar and Flat Rock Company.

No. 3117   **4000 shares.**

THIS IS TO CERTIFY, That _____ is entitled to one Share in the CAPITAL STOCK of said Company, created out of the Real Estate purchased in Brownstown, containing 703 50/100 acres, less or more, part of which is laid out into a town called 'GIBRALTAR,' and also of the village of 'VREELANDT,' and Mills and Water Privilege at Flat Rock,—all as now held by Joshua Howard, Benjamin B. Kercheval, and Peter Godfroy, as Trustees for said Company, subject however to the Articles of Association and By-Laws of said Company. This Certificate is assignable, by endorsement, but such transfer to be binding only when registered by the Secretary of said Association.

Given under the hands of the President and Secretary of said Association, at Detroit, this _____ day of _____ A. D. eighteen hundred and thirty _____

_____ Secretary.   _____ President.

Joshua Howard purchased 4,000 shares of Gibraltar and Flat Rock Canal Company stock on August 1, 1836. B. (Benjamin) Kercheval, president of the company, signed the document. Howard and Kercheval, trustees of the canal company, also platted Gibraltar in 1837. Because of promotions offered by the firm, the area filled with settlers.

The Blakely Tavern and Hotel, built by Alanson Parsons in 1836, was located on the corner of Washington (now Lowell) and Davis Streets. The building also housed the Bank of Gibraltar, which was chartered by a local group that included Joshua Howard. He was one of the more prominent investors in the Gibraltar and Flat Rock Land and Canal Company. Two prominent leaders associated with the enterprise were Lewis Cass and Daniel Webster. The canal company was located on the second floor of the hotel, and it is said that Webster made a fiery speech from the balcony about the great benefits to Michigan of the canal project. The bank operated for approximately nine months, but was forced to close because of depressed business conditions. The tavern was torn down in 1918.

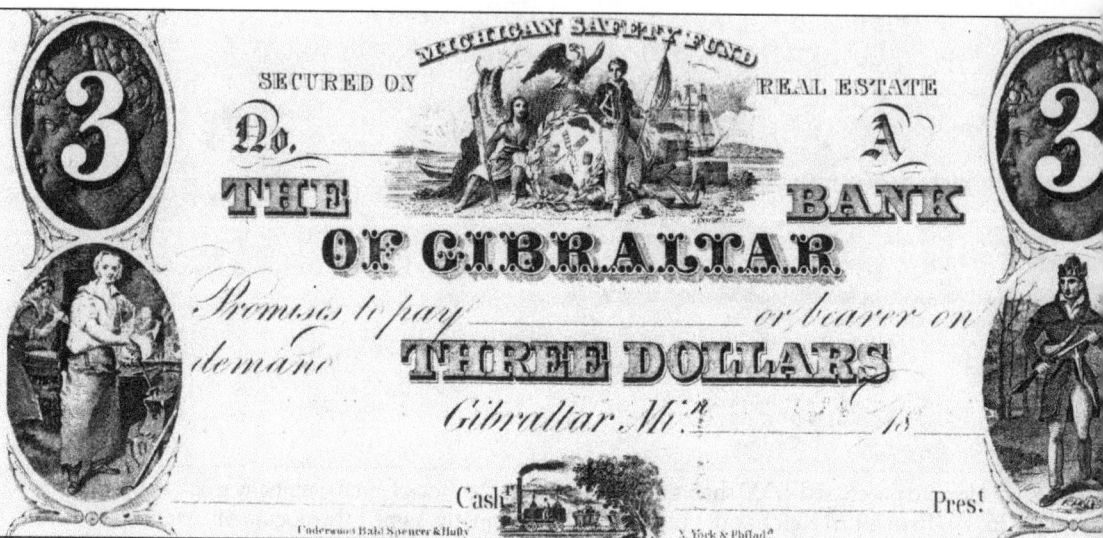

This $3 bill was printed by the Bank of Gibraltar in the 1830s. There were also denominations of $1, $2, and $5. In 1837, chartered banks were authorized to print and circulate their own money. Real estate held by the banks was used as collateral. This system invited the abusive practice of platting nonexistent towns and inflating the prices placed on the lots. The term "wildcat" was applied to the banks and the currency of this period. These procedures caused gradual depreciation of the banknotes, which in a short time became worthless.

The Gibraltar School and Church was built in 1845 by John Craig, one of the owners of the Linn and Craig shipyard. It was a grand building, with double doors and a winding staircase that led to the choir loft and organ. The church was of no denomination, and anyone was welcome to attend and preach. Below is a view of the inside of the classroom, with its potbellied stove. The teachers also served as janitors, and in the winter they had to keep the fire going in the stove. Mothers would help by bringing warm bricks to keep the children's feet warm.

This blurry photograph nevertheless provides a good idea of what Gibraltar looked like in the late 1800s. This view, looking north, is from the water tower on Adams Drive. The Gibraltar School and Church (left) was located on Warsaw Street, renamed Munro Street in 1954 after the Munro family of shipbuilders and captains. The dirt road that runs through the middle of this photograph is Adams Drive. William "Skip" Munro's home (center), located on the corner of Davis Street and Adams Drive, is still there today. (Courtesy Fay Blakely Steelman.)

A Ladies Aid was organized, and its members provided funds for the church. On January 12, 1911, it was noted that the Ladies Aid would pay what it could toward the minister's salary, which was $6 a month. The women's group held suppers and box socials to raise the funds. (Courtesy Fay Blakely Steelman.)

The one-room school held classes for kindergarten through eighth grade. Shown here is the class of 1912. If a funeral service was scheduled, school would be shut down for the day so the church facilities could be used. (Courtesy Fay Blakely Steelman.)

An annex was built onto the original school in 1935. Until that time, one teacher led all students, from kindergarten to eighth grade. One by one, teachers were added to the staff. The students then went to high school in neighboring Trenton. Some citizens recalled riding to school in a cattle car without windows for a year or two. (Courtesy Fay Blakely Steelman.)

The class of 1936 gathers for a photograph. Shown are, from left to right, (first row) Dorothy Law, Robert Morris, ? Sutton, unidentified, Donald Zea, and Ruth Law; (second row) Genevieve Fryer, ? Sutton, Dorothy Wright, Peggy Henderson, unidentified, Georgia Grostick, and Elsie McAughey; (third row) Frank McLenon, Billy Fickel, Earl Underwood, Jimmy McAughey, Ernest Wright, and Fay Blakely; (fourth row) Cleo Parsons (teacher), Ruth Denison, Mary Jean Grostick, unidentified, Audrey Labo, Betty Underwood, and Barbara Blakely; (fifth row) Donald Bell, Albert Wright, Jerry Jackson, Betty Denison, Betty Reabe, and Patricia Foster. (Courtesy Fay Blakely Steelman.)

On the steps of the old Gibraltar School and Church are, from left to right, teachers Cleo Parsons, Ethel Batten, Mrs. Broudhurst, and Mrs. Watts. Town social activities centered around the church and school. The PTA was active, holding monthly meetings and giving dinners to raise funds for improvements to the school. Lillian Fisher of Island Drive represented the elementary school at the school board. Due to her efforts, the school received playground equipment and needed supplies. (Courtesy Julie Storm.)

Bill Goss, the school janitor, would flood the skating rink in the winter. The rink was next to the school, and everyone was allowed to skate during the one-hour lunch. Behind the skaters in this c. 1938 photograph are the backs of the Chaney estate and the Springstead home. The homes would be facing Adams Drive. (Courtesy Ross Denison.)

The post office was established in Gibralter, as the town name was spelled at the time, on October 2, 1837, and was discontinued on January 31, 1910. The town's name was changed to Woodbury for a short time and then was changed back to Gibralter. Then, on December 19, 1900, the name was changed to the current version, Gibraltar. The city of Gibraltar had a substation for the Rockwood post office from the 1940s until the early 1980s. It was located in Arnold Kuster's store on the corner of Adams Drive and Stoeflet Street and later moved to the drugstore. Many people did not have a telephone and used the public phone at Kuster's.

United States Post Office

Gibraltar, Wayne County, Michigan

Established as Gibralter on October 2, 1837

Name changed to Woodbury on December 8, 1838

Name changed to Gibralter on May 13, 1839

Name changed to Gibraltar on December 19, 1900

Discontinued on January 31, 1910

Postmasters	Dates of Appointment
Almon Dunbar	October 2, 1837
William Munger	July 28, 1838
Michael O. Donovan	December 8, 1838
Alanson Parsons	May 13, 1839
Hiram Blakely	October 23, 1845
Eli W. Parsons	December 16, 1856
John M. Alford	September 19, 1864
John Dye	November 14, 1866
Robert Linn	November 28, 1866
William Spears	May 17, 1887
Edmund L. Denison	March 29, 1890
Charles E. Springstead	May 23, 1894
Joseph Alford	January 18, 1899
Nellie E. Davis	December 5, 1900
Nellie E. Denison	December 19, 1900

The Denison general store and post office was located on the southwest corner of Farnsworth Road (now Middle Gibraltar Road) and Adams Drive. The first telephone was in this store by 1903. A telephone sign hangs on the right side of the porch in the below photograph from 1903. (Courtesy Ross Denison.)

William Henry Denison (right) was born in Connecticut in 1819. After a short stay in California, he returned east via the South, working at a shipyard in Mississippi during the Civil War. He moved north to Brest, Michigan, and worked as a commercial fisherman. Denison accepted the job of lighthouse keeper in Gibraltar and moved there with his family around 1876. In the below photograph, his wife, Maria Stoddard Denison, is sitting on the porch of the Denison General Store and Post Office. (Courtesy Ross Denison.)

Edmund Denison was the son of William and Maria Denison. At left, he is picking up the mail at the Michigan Central train tracks on September 27, 1907. Edmund was the postmaster from March 1890 to May 1894. His wife, Nellie Blakely, pictured below, was postmistress from December 1900 until the post office was discontinued on January 31, 1910. (Courtesy Ross Denison.)

Cornelius Springstead was one of the earliest-known settlers, arriving in the area in 1818. He served as director of the school board in 1854. His brother Charles E. Springstead was a postmaster, serving from June 23, 1894, to January 18, 1899. This photograph of the Springstead home was taken in 1976, when Bill Reabe was the owner. The home, on Adams Drive, is still there today.

Another old family name in Gibraltar is Reabe. Their house, located on Adams Drive, was built in 1840 and is still a private residence today. The Reabe family owned farmland where the old McLouth Steel building is located today.

John MacArthur's home is located on Adams Drive. MacArthur owned a basket shop in the late 1800s. The shop was located on Washington Street, what is now Lowell Street. This photograph was taken in 1976.

The A.F. Buchner & Sons Grocery and Meat Market was established in 1915 and located on Adams Drive. Allen Terry purchased the store in 1937 and enlarged it. Many residents have memories of buying penny candy there. In the early 1960s, Joanne Davis and her daughter Linda Gerow purchased the store from Allen Terry. It became Jo-Lynne's Beauty Shop, named after Joanne and Linda. This photograph was taken in 1976. The beauty shop was torn down around 1982.

Otto H. Townsend (left) and his sons established a neon sign company in 1934. It was the village's first industry. John Townsend (right), Otto's son, is working on the intricate job of shaping a tube. The man in the center is unidentified.

The Townsend Neon Sign Company was located in this barn at the southern end of Horse Island. The barn wall facing the river was lighted at night to show the company name and helped to guide boaters in from the lake. The company, still in business today, is now located in Rockwood, Michigan. Members of the Townsend family still live on Horse Island. (Courtesy Clive Taylor.)

In the 1930s, the Boy Scouts established a troop in Gibraltar. The first troop was organized under the Monroe Council of the Boy Scouts of America, with Eugene Gadille Sr. as scoutmaster. As shown in these photographs, during the Depression, the Boy Scouts performed their duty by collecting aluminum.

Two

SHIPS AND BOATS

Construction on the first lighthouse in Gibraltar started on March 3, 1837, when the US Congress appropriated $5,000 for construction. It was located on the corner of Jefferson and Webster Streets, what are now Grandview and Munro Streets. Coast Guard records show that extensive repairs were needed in 1868. In 1869, it was reported that the dwelling and tower were in very bad condition and that a new building was necessary. Alanson Parsons was the first lighthouse keeper.

Construction began on the second Gibraltar lighthouse on February 1, 1873. An appropriation of $10,000 was approved on June 10, 1872. The new building was constructed on the same land as the previous lighthouse. This second lighthouse was discontinued in 1879 and, in 1895, the buildings and grounds were sold at public auction and the lantern and iron stairway of the tower were removed. The lighthouse as it stands today, without the tower, is a private residence still located on the corner of Grandview and Munro Streets. The lantern room was used in construction of the South Bass Island, Ohio, lighthouse in 1897 and is still there today. Michael J. Vreeland (1838–1876) and his wife, Mary Helen Stoflet Vreeland (1843–1910), were the last lighthouse keepers here.

The second Gibraltar lighthouse was converted into a private residence. Jim and Marion Knight lived in the home at the time of this 1976 photograph. The tower had been torn down, but, except for a little refurbishing, the home remains the same today.

The area had an abundance of oak, beech, elm, and ash trees. Robert W. Linn and Capt. John Craig built their shipyard on the banks of the Detroit River at what are Lowell and Coral Streets today. Linn was born in Scotland and came to Gibraltar in 1841. He was a shipbuilder, lumber dealer, and general store proprietor. He also served as postmaster of Gibraltar from November 28, 1866, to May 17, 1887. Linn was joined by Craig, who was born in New York in 1838. Linn and Craig were pioneers in building merchant vessels in this area.

Edmund Denison is standing with "Rock" next to Robert Linn's home in the mid to late 1800s. The Linn home was one and a half stories tall and was surrounded by a picket fence. It was always kept neat and trim, and the yard was filled with myrtles, violets, and lilies of the valley. It was located on the edge of the Detroit River, close to the shipyard Linn owned. The location of this photograph is Lowell Street today. (Courtesy Ross Denison.)

LISTING OF VESSELS
BUILT AT GIBRALTAR SHIP YARDS
1863 — 1882.

NAME	RIG	TONNAGE	WHERE BUILT	BY WHOM	WHEN BUILT
runette	Barge	738	Gibraltar	Linn & Craig	1863
race Whitney	"	289	"	Calkins	1866
ane Ralston	"	260	"	"	1866
da Medora	Schooner	301	"	"	1867
anistique	Propeller	474	"	Linn & Craig	1867
olin Campbell	"	373	"	" " "	1869
rank	Propeller	55	"	Unknown	1870
no	Schooner	137	"	Alford	1871
ed Jacket	Propeller	92	"	Clark	1871
onohansett	"	573	"	Linn & Craig	1872
artford	Schooner	323	"	Morgan "	1873
andusky	Barge	571	"	Linn & Craig	1873
hawnee	"	571	"	" " "	1873
renton	Schooner	47	"	Unknown	1874
lpena	Propeller	369	"	Linn & Craig	1874
assasoit	Barge	950	"	" " "	1874
uperior	Propeller	855	"	" " "	1874
. B. Hayes	Propeller	?	"	" " "	1877
lcona	Propeller	723	"	Linn & Co.	1878
iawatha	Propeller	1399	"	Linn & Craig	1880
essie H.Farwell	"	1200	"	" " "	1881
scanaba	"	1160	"	" " "	1881
renton	Schooner	48	"	Alford	1882

++++++++++++++++++++

This list of vessels includes all craft (steam or sail) built at the Gibraltar shipyards from 1863 to 1882. All information was obtained from the R.L. Polk & Company Marine Directory, published in 1884. The Monohansett was built in Gibraltar in 1872. It caught fire and sank near Alpena, Michigan. The wreckage is still visible today, and the Shipwreck Museum in Alpena offers tours. (Courtesy Fay Blakely Steelman.)

Joe Alford and his brother Charley were Gibraltar boatbuilders in the late 1800s and early 1900s. Joe, pictured here, was a postmaster from January 18, 1899, to December 1900. (Courtesy Fay Blakely Steelman.)

Joe Alford's house, pictured here in 1976, is still located on the corner of Adams Drive and Coral Street. The Gibraltar Firefighters Association bought the home for use as their clubhouse. It was named Fred Wall Hall in honor of retired firefighter Sgt. Fred Wall Sr., one of the first men to volunteer when the department organized in 1955. This home was also Elenore's Gift Shop at one time.

Brothers Joe and Charley Alford used to build layout and sneak boats as well as some small powerboats in an old barn (left) in back of Charley's house (right). In 1935, sneak boats were outlawed.

Joe and Charley Alford were the sons of Heman Alford. The house seen here became Charley's home. It is located on the corner of Adams Drive and Coral Street, across from Joe's home. This photograph was taken in 1976.

In 1866, the *Jane Ralston* was the first schooner built at the Linn and Craig shipyard in Gibraltar by builders John Drackett and Roderick Calkins. The *Jane Ralston*, named after Linn's mother, was a 137-foot wooden vessel. On July 21, 1910, on the west end of Lake Erie, the ship sprang a leak during a storm, became waterlogged, and sank. The hull was later raised and towed into Sandusky, Ohio, but was declared a total loss. (Courtesy Fay Blakely Steelman.)

This 1800s photograph shows the stern of the schooner *Oak Leaf*, owned by Capt. Daniel Munro (left), at the foot of Coral Street. Captain Munro was a long-waisted, six-foot, four-inch seafaring man who was always at the helm of the *Oak Leaf*.

This is another 1800s photograph of the *Oak Leaf*. The keel blocks still show in front of the old ship, moored here on the Detroit River at the end of Coral Street. Across the river in the background is Grosse Ile.

The 93-ton *Oak Leaf* measured 86 feet in length. It was one of the schooners built in Gibraltar at the Linn and Craig shipyard by the Munros. The ship was described as a trim little lady in black and green with a white belt. The *Oak Leaf* was built in 1895, the same year the *Charles Chambers* was constructed at Grosse Ile. These were the last trading schooners built on the Detroit River. The schooners hauled wood, sand, gravel, and coal from Gibraltar to Detroit. The *Oak Leaf* is seen here under full sail, coming back from Pointe Pelee, Canada, with gravel on its way to Ohio.

Three

PEOPLE WELL KNOWN ABOUT TOWN

Cleo Dillenbeck (June 1, 1881–April 16, 1965) was married to Lucius Parsons. She received her teaching certificate on August 22, 1903, and taught at the Gibraltar School for 35 years until her retirement in 1950. She was the only teacher who taught kindergarten to eighth grade in the one-room school until 1935, when the annex was built. (Courtesy Fay Blakely Steelman.)

A contest was held to choose a name for the new elementary school. Mary Jane Day won with her submission of Cleo E. Parsons. On July 22, 1959, the Gibraltar Board of Education passed a resolution to rename the new Gibraltar elementary school Cleo E. Parsons Elementary School, in honor of Parsons (pictured), whose influence for good upon the youth of the community has been incalculable. (Courtesy Fay Blakely Steelman.)

Cleo Parsons's former home is located on Adams Drive. It is a quaint clapboard-style house with gingerbread trim and a white picket fence. The Wall family purchased the home in 1968. Larry Wall, who served two terms as mayor of Gibraltar (November 13, 1979–November 14, 1983, and November 25, 1985–October 13, 1986), still lives in the home today.

This is a view of the Hall farm photographed from the Detroit River in 1961. The farmhouse is at center, with the carriage house and pump house to the left and the boat house to the right. Edmund Hall (May 28, 1819–May 17, 1903) was a very prominent figure in this area. He was a lawyer as well as a successful lumberman who built a large sawmill in Bay City, Michigan. He spent his summers on the large farm he had in Gibraltar. He owned all of the land that extended past Grandview Street. The farm contained his country house and a granary, icehouse, and blacksmith shop. He also had cattle that grazed along the banks of the Detroit River. The Hall farm still exists, although the property is much smaller and some of the outbuildings are now gone. (Courtesy Warren Heier Jr.)

Frederick Stoflet Hall, pictured here in 1930, was the only son of Edmund Hall and his second wife, Mary H. Vreeland (1843–1910). Stoflet was Mary's maiden name, and she was the widow of Col. Michael J. Vreeland (1838–1876). Edmund Hall's first wife was Emeline Cochran. He also had a daughter, Frances Chaney Strong.

In later years, a building behind Edmund Hall's house became the Patterson School. It was run by Hilda and Irene Patterson for about 10 years until 1955. The Patterson School, shown here, was a boarding school for children with learning disabilities and those assigned there by the court. They received some private funding and very little state aid.

William Munro, or Skip, as many called him (short for Skipper), was one of the last of the Great Lakes schooner captains. His father, Hector (1818–1884), a Gibraltar pioneer settler, was a carpenter, shipbuilder, and a schooner captain. He brought his wife, Ann, and seven children from Scotland to America, and they made their way to this tiny waterfront community around 1875 to work in the shipyards. The youngest of the seven was William (November 7, 1869–September 30, 1958). All of Hector's sons sailed the family's schooners. They would build the boats in the winter when the lakes were frozen and sail in the summer. (Courtesy Fay Blakely Steelman.)

This is the wedding photograph of William (Skip) Munro and Hattie Hanchett. They were married on January 26, 1898. The couple had three children, William Jr. and twins Hazen and Hazel. Skip's sailing days ended five years after their marriage, when Hattie died of typhoid pneumonia, leaving him with the children. William Jr. was five and the twins were 16 months old at the time of their mother's death. (Courtesy Fay Blakely Steelman.)

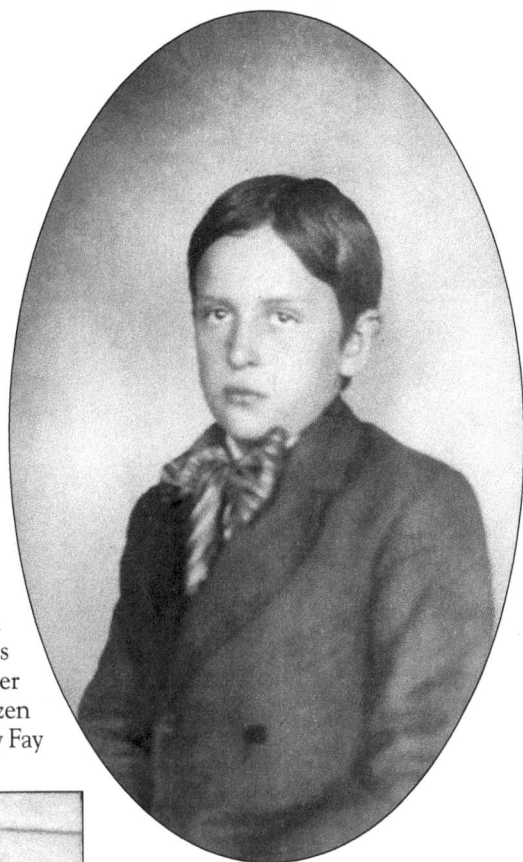

William Jr., seen at right, was Skip's oldest son. Skip Munro never remarried, and he raised his children by doing carpentry and working in the shipyards. He also served as Brownstown Township's justice of the peace for 25 years and as the supervisor of the township's water district for 30 years. The twins, Hazel and Hazen (below), were born on July 15, 1904. (Courtesy Fay Blakely Steelman.)

Shown here are, from left to right, William Jr., Eulalia Truax Hanchett (Hattie's mother and grandmother of the Munro children), Hazel, William Sr., and Hazen Munro. They are standing outside the family home. Eulalia, who helped with the children, was related to Abraham Truax and Giles Slocum of Trenton. The Detroit River is in the background. (Courtesy Fay Blakely Steelman.)

Skip and Hattie Munro's home, seen here in October 1919, is located on Adams Drive and the corner of Davis Street. The home is still there today, but the front door has been moved to the side of the house, off Davis Street. The home had a large anchor in the front yard. Hazen Munro moved it to the home he built on the corner of Lowell and Grandview Streets. (Courtesy Fay Blakely Steelman.)

Hattie had a small notions store next door to the Munro home on Adams Drive. She sold various items, including ice cream, candy, tobacco, and soft drinks. The store, seen here, has been remodeled and is a private residence today. (Courtesy Fay Blakely Steelman.)

Hazel Munro (daughter of Hattie Hanchett) is sitting on the fender of the car next to her friend in this 1920s photograph. They are sitting at the site of her family home on Davis Street and Adams Drive. The water tower on Adams Drive is visible behind the car. Fay Blakely Steelman, who has contributed many photographs and family history to this book, is the eldest daughter of Hazel Munro. Her sisters are Barbara and Elaine. (Courtesy Fay Blakely Steelman.)

Skip's older brother Daniel Munro (far right), another Munro sea captain, poses with his family at their home on Lowell Street. Daniel Munro lived next door to Robert Linn, one of the owners of the Linn and Craig shipyard.

Hazen and Hazel Munro, seen here with their father, Skip, were not without accomplishment. Hazel, who was married to Fred Blakely and owned the Gibraltar Boat Yard, was a Gibraltar historian. And Hazen, known as "Scotch," was civic-minded, serving four terms on the Gibraltar City Council and as a member of the city's charter commission. (Courtesy Fay Blakely Steelman.)

VILLAGE OF GIBRALTAR

GIBRALTAR, MICHIGAN

BE IT RESOLVED: That the name of Warsaw Street
within the limits of the Village be herewith changed to
Munro Avenue.

WHEREAS: The name of Warsaw Street within the
Village limits is undesirable and

WHEREAS: The Village is desirable of the changing
the name thereof to Munro Avenue as a tribute to William Munro Sr.
and all the members of the Munro family who have figured so
prominently in the History of Gibraltar.

Joseph L. Collins

Joseph L. Collins, Clerk
Village of Gibraltar.

Dated: December 20, 1954.

We take this opportunity to wish the
Munro family a very MERRY CHRISTMAS and HAPPY NEW YEAR.

FROM ALL THE OFFICERS OF THE VILLAGE.

This resolution, dated December 20, 1954, is to change the name of Warsaw Street to Munro Avenue, after William (Skip) Munro Sr. and all of the members of the Munro family. The old school/church was located on Warsaw Street, as were Gibraltar's first municipal buildings. Today, the new city municipal complex is also located on Munro Avenue.

Hy Dahlka was many things during his lifetime in Gibraltar. Besides being the first village president, he was very involved with wildlife conservation. He was founder of the Michigan United Conservation Club (MUCC) in 1937. Dahlka (right) shakes hands with Michigan governor G. Mennen Williams at a MUCC meeting in Owosso in the 1950s. (Courtesy Fred Wall.)

Everything in Hy Dahlka's life was centered on the water. Hy and his brother Kenneth spent their youth hunting, fishing, and boating along the lower Detroit River and upper Lake Erie. As adults, they earned their living from the water. The Dahlka Dredging Company was owned by Hy Dahlka. He is seen here dredging out the canals and boat slips at Heinrich Marina in the late 1950s.

Layout boats are anchored in the Detroit River. Celeron Island is seen in the upper left, and the boathouse on the Hall farm is in the upper center of this 1950s photograph taken from Hy Dahlka's yard. Dahlka was a lifelong Gibraltar resident with a national reputation as a sportsman and an authority on layout shooting techniques and the Gibraltar area marshes. (Courtesy Fred Wall.)

This photograph of Hy Dahlka's home was taken from the Detroit River in September 1958. The home was moved from Monroe, Michigan, in 1945. It was floated on a barge to its current location on Lowell Street at the end of Coral Street. This location was formerly the Linn and Craig shipyard. Hy passed away in 1983 at age 79. Hy's daughter Sandy and her husband, Fred Wall, still live in the home today. (Courtesy Fred Wall.)

A member of the Migratory Bird Committee, Hy Dahlka (left) is in his basement in December 1946 banding wintering and spring migratory ducks. This research provided invaluable information. (Courtesy Fred Wall.)

Four

IT IS ALL
ABOUT THE WATER

This postcard of "Pointe of Pretty Gibraltar" was postmarked August 14, 1914, and was mailed to Elizabeth Benjamin of Cherry Street in Wyandotte, Michigan. The back of the house is on a canal, and the front faces the river, locating this house on Horse Island.

SCENE AT GIBRALTAR ON THE WATER

19 Miles from Detroit City Hall—Paved Roads Any Route

Where Lake and River Meet   Free Picnic Grounds in Virgin Forest

In this 1920s postcard, the view is to the south and Lake Erie. The Detroit River is on the left. Celeron Island is in the upper left corner.

SCENE AT GIBRALTAR ON THE WATER

Where Lake and River Meet   Free Picnic Grounds in Virgin Forest

This 1920s postcard is of Adams Drive looking south. Adams Drive curves right and then meets with Bayview Street. Where both roads connect is the southern tip of Hall Island, which was a park and picnic area. (Courtesy Fay Blakely Steelman.)

This photograph of Gibraltar, taken from the water tower, looks north. Adams Drive is on the left and the Detroit River is on the right. The pier in the river is the location of the Linn and Craig shipyard. It was quite a long pier, having 1,200 to 1,500 pilings. The Humbug Marsh is beyond that. (Courtesy Fay Blakely Steelman.)

This 1920s photograph of Adams Drive is looking north. The end of the dirt road is the current location of Humbug Marina. In the foreground at left is the Springstead home. Beyond it is the Chaney estate without its stone wall. On the right side of the photograph is the Reabe home. (Courtesy Fay Blakely Steelman.)

The map shows the route to reach Gibraltar, with labeled locations including DETROIT, DEARBORN, MICHIGAN AV., SPRINGWELLS, FORD ROUGE PLANT, OAKWOOD BLVD., MELVINDALE, ECORSE RD., LINCOLN PARK, FORDVILLE, EUREKA RD., WYANDOTTE, RIVERVIEW, SIBLEY, WEST RD., TRENTON, ELIZABETH PARK, S. GIBRALTAR RD., FLAT ROCK, ROCKWOOD, HURON RIVER, TELEGRAPH RD., TOLEDO, DIXIE HIGHWAY, FORT ST., JEFFERSON AV., DETROIT RIVER, FIGHTING ISLE, GROSSE ISLE, HALL'S GIBRALTAR PROPERTIES, HORSE ISLE, BROWNSTON BAY, LAKE ERIE

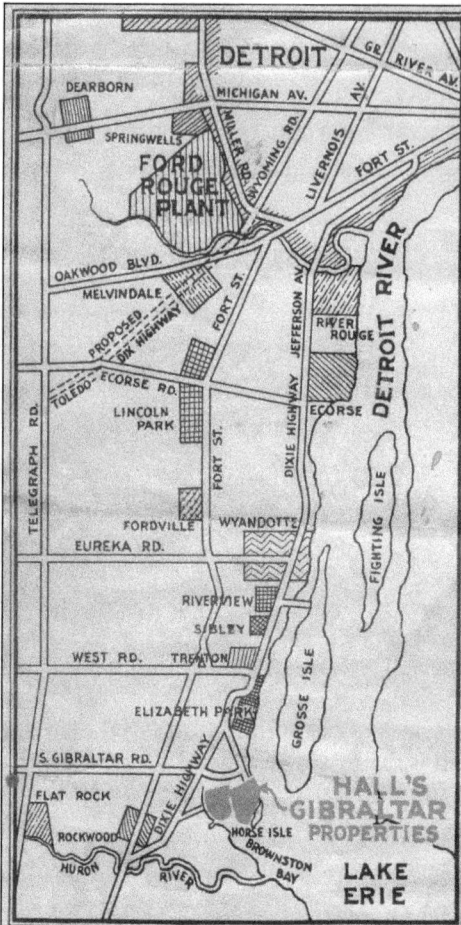

HOW TO REACH GIBRALTAR

MAIL THE COUPON

LEINBACH BROTHERS & CO.
730 Buhl Building, Detroit.
Dear Sirs:—Please mail full particulars about Gibraltar.

Name ....

Address .... Phone ....

ASK FOR SALESMAN

~ HALL'S ~
GIBRALTAR

Detroit River
All Year
HOMESITES

During the 1920s, real estate brokers Leinbach Brothers & Company were trying to sell lots in Gibraltar. The firm boasted in its brochure about the good duck shooting near Detroit, the ideal conditions for motor- and speed-boating, and the investment value of a purchase in Gibraltar. The Leinbach Brothers realty office was on the corner of Adams and Island Drive. The Houseman-Spitzley Corporation was another real estate broker interested in Gibraltar at that time. (Courtesy Norman Gerow.)

68

Between 1925 and 1932, Gibraltar's location at the Detroit River and the marshes surrounding it offered a prime spot for rum-running during Prohibition. This small building was located on the north end of Lowell Street and built closer to the back of the lot. It is said that it was built and used as a strategically placed lookout point during the days of rum-running. Before the marinas were built on North and Middle Gibraltar Roads, one could see approaching cars and be ready to signal a warning to those engaged in the illegal operation.

Boats like this Hacker with a Packard engine were made for rum-running. Here, Warren Heier looks out of the window of his new boat in the canal off of Bayview Drive in May 1932. The Detroit River would freeze over, and rumrunners would drive to Canada and back, leaving the car door open just in case the car went through the ice. There were also a few cabarets operating in Gibraltar at that time. (Courtesy Warren Heier Jr.)

Hall Island (sometimes called Main), the largest of the Gibraltar islands, is seen here in 1958. Many of the first homes built in Gibraltar were summer cottages. During the Depression, however, as many people lost their homes in the city, and as the market for summer homes faded, many of these cottages became permanent homes. Gibraltar has two faces, one from the road and one from the water. Seeing the community from a boat makes it clear why Gibraltar is called "The Venice of Michigan."

In 1920, there were roughly 20 permanent homes and a few summer cottages in Gibraltar. The first private home on Hall Island, or Little Snake Island, as it was known at that time, was built by the family of Marie Halbeisen in 1923. There was no gas, water, or electricity, and the canal across the street from their home was not dredged until 1928.

Marie Halbeisen, who never married, was known in the neighborhood by most people as Miss Halbeisen. She is seen here riding in the Fourth of July parade in 1974. Miss Halbeisen started the Garden Club in 1950.

In this 1950s photograph, a boater takes a leisurely cruise down one of the many canals in Gibraltar. Homes on Pointe Drive are visible in the background. Most of the islands were lined with weeping willows along the canals before the area was built up. Willows were used because their root system offered great erosion control.

Edmund Island (or Triangle, as it is known locally) is seen in this 1958 aerial photograph. To the left is Hall Island, and to the right is Cherry Island, which is now part of the Lake Erie Metropark.

In 1929, Dr. Vasik, a dentist, was the first to build a home on what was called Big Snake Island, now Edmund (Triangle) Island. This large brick house is still at the southeast end of the island.

In the 1920s, Horse Island, formerly owned by Frances Chaney Strong, Edmund Hall's daughter, was platted and the lots sold for building. Most of the lots were bought for summer cottages. This 1958 aerial photograph of Horse Island shows Hall Island on the left. The Detroit River, on the right of the island, opens into Lake Erie at the end of Horse Island. From Horse Island, beyond this photograph, points north include Trenton East to Grosse Ile, Celeron Island, and Canada. To the south is Lake Erie.

The upper half of this 1958 photograph shows the main part of Gibraltar and a new subdivision being developed. The street closest to the Detroit River is Lowell Street. The area closest to the river was Gibraltar proper from 1854 to 1899.

Charles Nichols was one of Gibraltar's first councilmen, in 1954. His home is located on a canal on Worth Street, which is in the main part of the city. This residence, still standing today, was purchased in 1937 from the Houseman-Spitzley Corporation, a real estate firm that was developing subdivisions in Gibraltar. (Courtesy Julie Storm.)

The Horse Island Bridge is seen here in the 1950s before it was paved. The small arch bridge has one of the most unique appearances of any bridge in the state of Michigan. It features a steep arch, making it look more like an old European footbridge than a 1920s vehicular concrete arch bridge. No other bridge in the state follows this design. It retains near-perfect historical integrity due to its unique and attractive design and the low traffic volume it experiences on the residential dead-end road. The bridge was listed in the Historic Bridge Inventory and is eligible for listing in the National Register of Historic Places.

Another historic bridge is on Middle Gibraltar Road. It was built in 1932 by the Wayne County Road Commissioners. A main canal runs between the mainland and Hall Island. Flanking the 38-foot roadway are two five-and-a-half-foot-wide sidewalks. The concrete railing has urn-shaped spindles. The bottom of the bridge is curved to suggest an arched structure, making the bridge an attractive focal point for the surrounding village. Heinrich Marina (now Humbug Marina) is on the north side of the bridge. The 1931–1932 annual report of the Wayne County road commissioners noted that "this low sweeping arch bridge is in keeping with its surroundings and is one of the features which make Gibraltar Road so attractive." This bridge is an excellent example of the attractive and creative designs developed by the road commission.

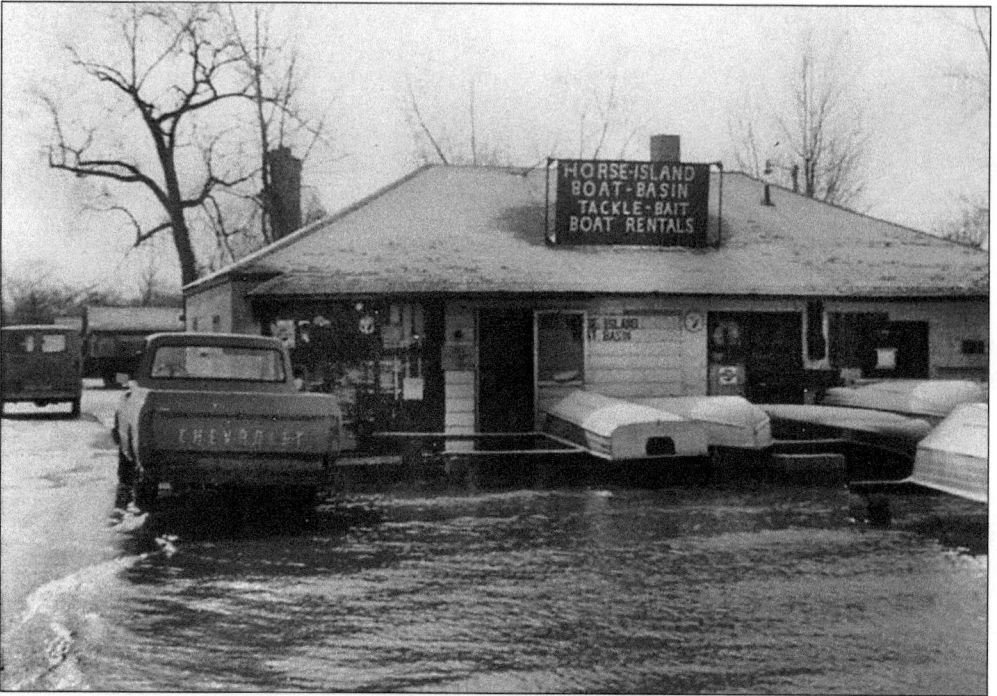

The Horse Island Boat Basin was owned by the Tennant family in the 1960s. It was a small, cinderblock building. The Tennants rented fishing boats and boat wells. They also sold bait. (Courtesy Tamey Gorris.)

Boats are docked at the Horse Island Boat Basin. In the background, across the canal, are homes on Adams Drive. Visible in the canal between the boat basin and Adams Drive is a small island. Years of high water and floods washed pieces of the island away until it completely disappeared. (Courtesy Tamey Gorris.)

Ella Vick, or Queenie, as she was known, is seen at right standing by the door of Vick's Boat Livery on Horse Island. The livery was located in the garage across the street from her home that she owned in 1945. There was a boat ramp and a few docks that she rented, and she also sold bait. Her granddaughter Bonnie, along with Bonnie's cousins, would help when they could. Bonnie remembers her cousins picking night crawlers at the Grosse Isle Golf Course for bait. The boat livery was next to the Horse Island Boat Basin. Below, Queenie stands on one of the boat docks. The Horse Island Bridge can be seen in the background. (Courtesy Bonnie Dougherty.)

William Heinrich built the Heinrich Marina in 1954. It was a large swamp area when he purchased the property from William Lawson. After a few years of dredging, Heinrich was able to construct about 100 boat wells. In the upper center of the above photograph is the marina office, with the Gibraltar police boat in the hoist. To the right is the historical bridge on Middle Gibraltar Road. Below is the gas dock at the marina. (Courtesy William Heinrich.)

During the holidays in the early 1960s, the Heinrich Marina displayed a silver Christmas tree in the window. There weren't many streetlights at this time, and the sparkling silver tree could be seen quite well. (Courtesy William Heinrich.)

The Heinrich Marina is seen beyond one of Gibraltar's historic bridges. This span, on Middle Gibraltar Road, crosses over the main canal to Hall Island. (Courtesy William Heinrich.)

In the 1950s, the Humbug Club, a duck-hunting club, was located in this marsh overlooking the Detroit River. This property later became part of the Humbug Marina. (Courtesy Sue Crider.)

Everett Hedke purchased the Heinrich Marina in 1964 and started to expand it by dredging and adding more docks and boat-storage buildings. Adams Drive was closed off at Middle Gibraltar Road and was made the entrance to the expanded marina. (Courtesy Sue Crider.)

Humbug Marina, seen here in 1987, does not look much different from its early beginnings as the Heinrich Marina, except for the fact that it became a large commercial marina with many more docks and large storage buildings. It has rack storage in another section of the marina, known as Humbug Too. (Courtesy Sue Crider)

In 1968, at Humbug Marina, Everett Hedke was contracted to build a meticulous reproduction of the paddleboat *Suwanee* for Greenfield Village. Here, Fred Wall (right) and some helpers are working on the paddleboat. It was the first major boat built in Gibraltar since 1895. The original *Suwanee* was a 25-ton, 56-foot paddle-wheel boat on the Mississippi River. The first *Suwanee's* old pilothouse and controls were installed in the replica.

After the *Suwanee* was finished, it was just a bit too wide to get out of the building, so some of the wall needed to be trimmed off. Everett Hedke (left) is watching the operation. (Courtesy the collections of The Henry Ford.)

Barely clearing the overpass, the *Suwanee* makes her way back to Greenfield Village after being completed in March 1970 at Humbug Marina. (Courtesy the collections of The Henry Ford.)

The *Suwanee* was a longstanding feature at Greenfield Village (The Henry Ford) in Dearborn, Michigan. However, it has now been dry-docked due to extensive repairs and lack of funding.

Humbug Marina also served as a dock for the smaller Bob Lo boats, such as the *Tecumseh*. The Bob Lo Island Amusement Park operated from 1898 to 1993. It was located on Bois Blanc Island, Ontario, Canada, just above the mouth of the Detroit River. In 1984, the Gibraltar dock opened. (Courtesy Sue Crider.)

This pavilion sheltered passengers as they waited to board the Bob Lo ferry. The Bob Lo amusement park closed on September 30, 1993. The pavilion, unused since then, is waiting to be moved to its new location, where it will be renovated for community events. (Courtesy Sue Crider.)

Other forms of water entertainment were the boat parades. Boaters would decorate their vessels and parade through the canals of Gibraltar. Prizes were given out for the best decorations. (Above, courtesy Fay Blakely Steelman; below, courtesy Clive Taylor.)

In 1970, a boat race was held on Lowell Street. Racers were able to launch their boats right off of Lowell Street, as there were no seawalls at the time. This photograph was taken from Hy Dahlka's property, looking south. (Courtesy Clive Taylor.)

For Michigan Week in the 1950s, big celebrations were held. A parade of decorated boats navigated through the canals. Pictured here are the Boat King and Queen.

White limestone was mined from the old quarry and used as ballast for ships and the foundation for the lighthouse. It was also loaded into rail cars after being crushed, to be used in the making of steel and iron. Frederick Stoflet Hall once owned the quarry. It was located next to the train depot at the MC tracks that cross Gibraltar Road. Frederick sold the quarry in 1934. During the 1970s, the old limestone quarry was the site of swimming and summer picnics.

The quarry was part of the land purchased by the McLouth Steel Corporation. McLouth offered to lease the quarry to Gibraltar for a token sum. However, the city was unable to obtain the necessary liability insurance to operate the quarry. The quarry was then closed. When it was drained, many items were found at the bottom, including class rings.

In the 1920s, a canal was dredged along the eastern edge of the Blakely property. Beginning as a hobby in the late 1930s, Fred Blakely starting creating facilities where friends and relatives could haul out their boats for the winter. By the early 1940s, this became a part-time business for Blakely, and in 1946, the Gibraltar Boat Yard, owned by Blakely and Hazen Munro, was in business. Fred left his job at Detroit Edison in the early 1950s and continued to expand the marina until 1968. The marina is located on North Gibraltar Road. (Courtesy Fay Blakely Steelman.)

Fred Blakely is standing by one of the gas pumps at the Gibraltar Boat Yard. He started with about 20 boat wells and later added additional gas pumps, marine accessories, and parts. (Courtesy Fay Blakely Steelman.)

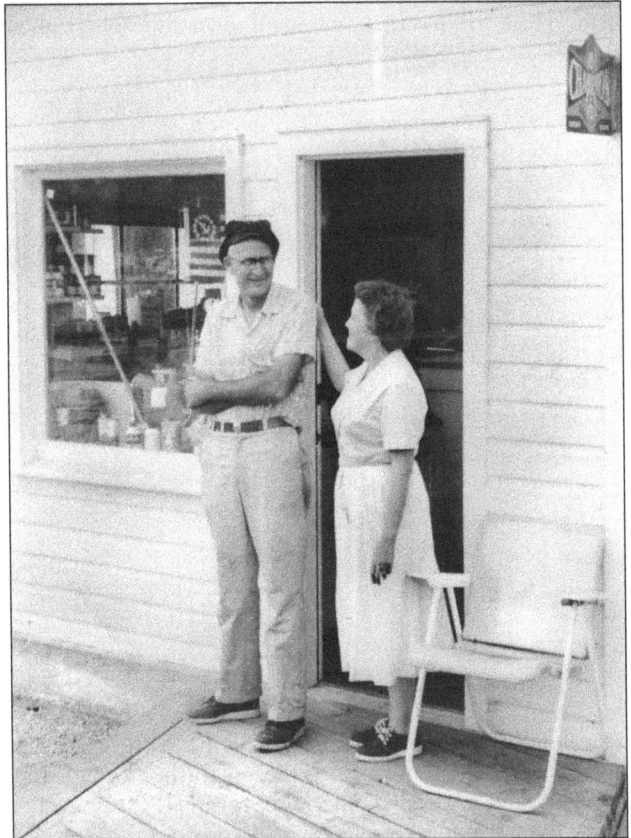

Fred Blakely and his wife, Hazel (Munro), stand in the doorway of the Gibraltar Boat Yard office in the 1960s. They sold the marina to Jack Buhl in 1968. (Courtesy Fay Blakely Steelman.)

Jack Buhl has owned the Gibraltar Boat Yard since 1968. Over the years, changes have been made, but it still has the same small-town atmosphere about it.

The canals are very picturesque, and living by the water is a slow and easy lifestyle. However, the floods of 1972 tell another story. Most of the homes on Pointe Drive (Hall Island) were built below flood level, as evidenced in these photographs. In some homes, water came up to the middle of living room windows. (Courtesy Clive Taylor.)

This is the major intersection of downtown Gibraltar. On the left is the local grocery store, located on the corner of Middle Gibraltar and South Gibraltar Roads. There are apartment buildings next to it and, beyond them, homes. (Courtesy Clive Taylor.)

The Evacuation Ducks were purchased in 1955 for the Village of Gibraltar for the evacuation of residents of the Gibraltar Islands in the event of an emergency. The three amphibious trucks, known as "ducks," have found many uses in the village. Assigned to the police and fire departments and the Department of Public Works, they have been painted in distinctive identifiable colors and have been helpful in patrolling the waters of the Detroit River. One of them is equipped with high-pressure pumps for accessory fire protection. A duck is seen here in 1972 on Adams Drive, rescuing residents from flooded areas. They have been used for lighter purposes as well, such as for recreation hayrides. (Courtesy Clive Taylor.)

Fred Wall is driving one of the amphibious trucks, or ducks, crossing the Detroit River. He is following another duck coming back from Celeron Island to Gibraltar in September 1958. It was possible at the time to drive the ducks in and out of the water off of Lowell Street, since there was no seawall there. Wall's passenger, facing the camera, is Roy Westphal, first Department of Public Works director. (Courtesy Fred Wall.)

The above photograph shows the dikes built along the water's edge by the Army Corps of Engineers in 1973. The dikes were several feet high and limited the view of the water from most homes. This dike is running along Lowell Street. The Detroit River is on the other side of the dike, and Celeron Island is in the background. The below photograph shows the Horse Island Bridge and the dike constructed on the right side of it. The dikes remained until the wood frames rotted and fell or the property owners tore them down, preferring the view of the water to the protection from a potential flood. The floods in 1985 convinced homeowners to construct clay dikes, built by the city in 1986. (Courtesy Bonnie Doherty)

Five

A MAJOR INDUSTRY COMES TO GIBRALTAR

In 1954, this is what the future site of the McLouth Steel Company looked like. The farmland, once owned by the Reabe family, is located on West Jefferson Road between Vreeland and Middle Gibraltar Roads. McLouth bought 4.3 square miles of Gibraltar to build a stainless steel mill. Gibraltar was flat broke at this time, and there were no police, fire, or public service departments, just a few paved roads and no sewers. But loans from the state and Brownstown Township got things going until the steel plant was able to start paying taxes. (Courtesy Robert Wright.)

TO THE MEMORY OF THOSE BURIED IN ST. JOSEPH CEMETERY, GIBRALTAR, MICHIGAN, 1855–1911. THE REINTERMENT OF 207 REMAINS MADE HERE, JANUARY, 1965.

Before construction of the McLouth Steel plant was to begin, Downriver's oldest Catholic cemetery needed to be evacuated. The cemetery was located on the west side of River Road, what is now called West Jefferson and North Gibraltar Road. It was on McLouth property, and McLouth agreed to pay for the costs of reinterment to Our Lady of Hope Cemetery in Brownstown. (Courtesy Jim Koerber.)

Building McLouth Steel brought much hope to this area. Construction of the new steel mill was started in 1954. (Courtesy Robert Wright)

McLouth Steel was looking to expand its operations closer to the river. North Gibraltar Road ran straight through the property the company needed to achieve this. So, McLouth closed off part of North Gibraltar Road and constructed the new section right through the Denison farm. The home was moved, but the barn was torn down. Here, Ross Denison and his wife (at left) watch the construction. (Courtesy Ross Denison.)

The northern end of North Gibraltar Road was closed off. The new section of the road curved to complete the thoroughfare. Where the Denison home was once located is now the Marina Bay apartment complex. (Courtesy Ross Denison.)

McLouth Steel was sold to Detroit Steel Company in 1996. It is now owned by Steel Rolling Holdings. The steel plant operates today, but on a much smaller scale. (Courtesy Robert Wright.)

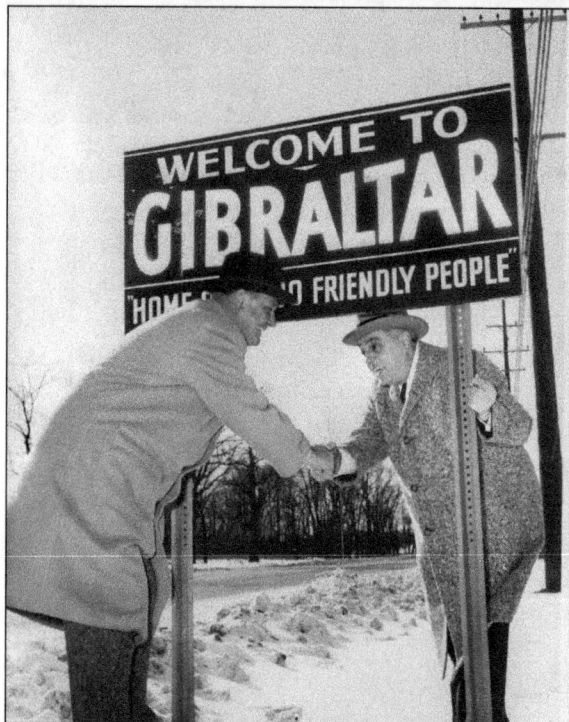

Gibraltar was incorporated as a village in 1954, virtually overnight, by the efforts of several people who finished collecting signatures during the night on a petition to form a village. The petition was presented to the state capital when it opened in the morning. Up to that time, Gibraltar was a part of Brownstown, and Trenton had intentions to annex the McLouth property. Village president Hy Dahlka (right) is seen here shaking hands with neighboring city Trenton's mayor, Ken Dahlka, his brother.

Members of the first city council are, from left to right, Howard Burt, Jim Walsh, Fred Williams, Cam Poleski, Charles Nichols, and Ross Denison. Seated in front is village president Hy Dahlka. This same council would be in office when Gibraltar became a city in 1961.

The governor of Michigan, G. Mennen "Soapy" Williams (center), signs a copy of the village of Gibraltar charter, given to C.W. Bertwhistle as a member of the charter commission. The signing is witnessed by village president Hy Dahlka (right) and village attorney Raleigh Raubolt.

Ivan Ransford was a patrolman in neighboring Trenton for two years before he was chosen in September 1954 to start the police and fire services in newly incorporated Gibraltar. He was the village's first police chief and fire chief and was alone with a gun, badge, and policeman's handbook. He now had the responsibility to protect 1,800 people and patrol 4.3 square miles.

The Gibraltar Police and Rescue boat was purchased in 1956. It was too large to be used between the bridges. The people who lived on the canals felt they had a real problem with speeding boats washing their yards away. On the other hand, the larger boat was useful in rescuing or helping to tow stranded boaters.

When the old Gibraltar school and church burned down in 1954, all that remained was the annex, which had been built in 1935. This annex later became the Gibraltar Municipal Building, which was used until the new Municipal Complex was built in 2004.

The Gibraltar Fire Department is attached to the Municipal Building. Shown here is the department's squad of vehicles in the late 1950s.

This photograph of Gibraltar's firemen was taken for Firemen's Field Day on September 22, 1957, in Monroe, Michigan. Shown are, from left to right (kneeling) Bob Heumann, Wilford "Blackie" Shown, Art Beauman, and Fred Wall; (standing) John "Red" Cooney, Art Redman, Charles Seabrook, Chief Ivan Ransford, Larry Loomis, and Bernie McVickers. (Courtesy Gibraltar Firefighters Association.)

In 1961, the Gibraltar village residents voted to become a city. The new charter called for a department of public safety. The three employees who were hired as firemen and the four men employed as police officers were reassigned, and all became public safety officers.

The Gibraltar Department of Public Works is located on the corner of Munro Avenue and Coral Street. It was built in 1958, across the street from the Municipal Building and the public safety department.

On July 21, 1961, Gibraltar was incorporated as a city with a population of 2,187, making it the second-smallest city in Michigan. Charles Shumate, serving as president of the village, returned as the first mayor, and all six councilmen elected the previous year were returned to office.

Helen Shumate, the wife of Mayor Charles Shumate, was a gym teacher at Parsons Elementary School. She later became the principal of Oscar A. Carlson High School. Shumate Junior High was named after her.

Gibraltar's downtown area consisted mainly of this complex, located on the corner of Middle and South Gibraltar Roads. In 1958, Bob Mower built the pharmacy, grocery store, and laundromat. His brother Dick built the professional building that housed a barbershop, beauty shop, and the offices of Dr. Laurence Klein and Dr. Edwin Greszik. Shown here is the annual clean-up day in May 1970.

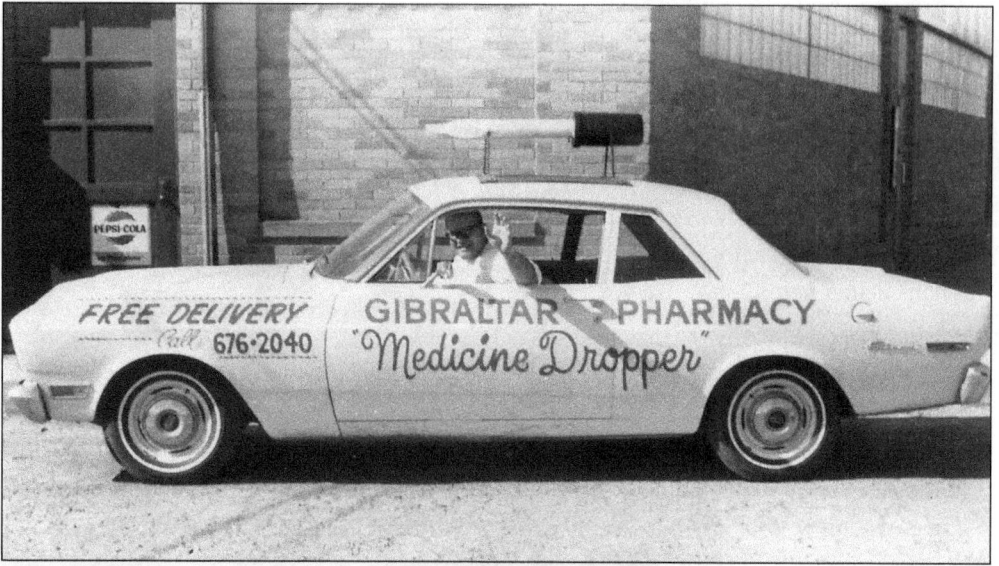

Ralph Freeman was the pharmacist at the Rexall Pharmacy. He is waving from his delivery car, complete with medicine dropper on the roof, in the parking lot of the Rexall Pharmacy. In 1958, this was Shepherds Drug Store. (Courtesy Ralph Freeman.)

Don Comella, owner of Don's Barber Shop, stands inside his establishment in the 1980s. The shop was on the backside of the complex. He operated the barbershop for 38 years, from May 1966 to May 2004, when the complex was torn down. (Courtesy Don Comella.)

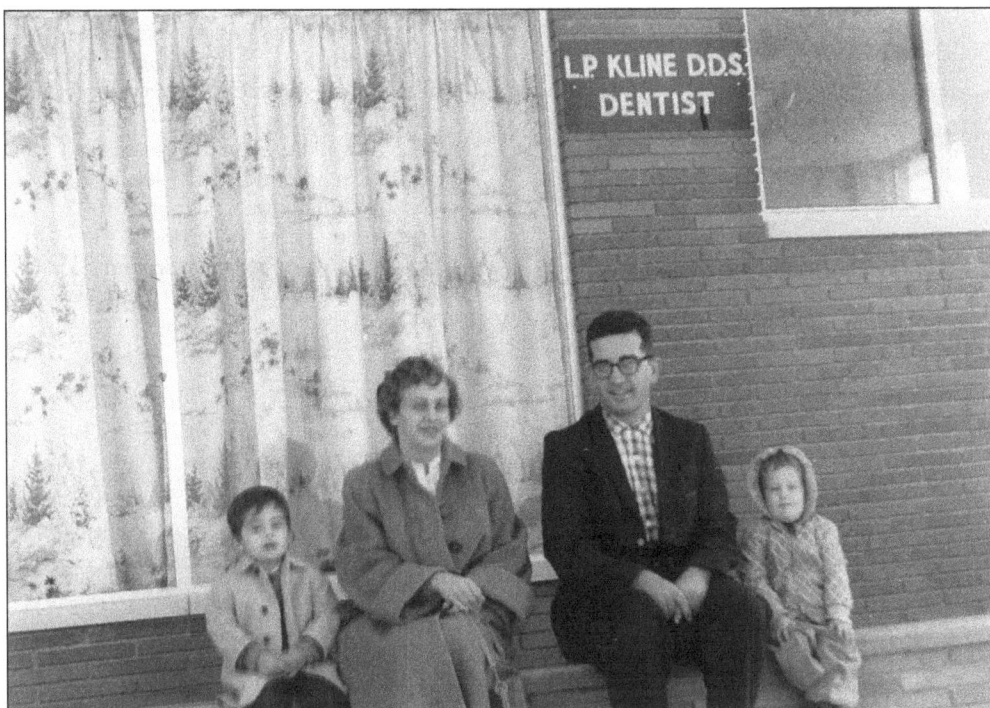

Sitting in front of his new office in 1960 is Dr. Kline with his wife, Joann, and their two sons. Dr. Kline was the first to rent the brand-new office. In later years, he purchased the professional building. His dental practice was there until 2004, when the complex was torn down. (Courtesy Joann Kline.)

The Sinclair gas station was built by Jack Lawrence in 1958. In the fall of that year, Larry Champion was the first to lease the new station, located on the corner of North Gibraltar and Middle Gibraltar Roads. It was called Champs Sinclair Service Station. (Courtesy Linda Bromund.)

The Sinclair gas station tow truck is parked outside of Larry Champion's home on the corner of Fryer and Stoeflet Streets. The view is looking toward Middle Gibraltar Road. Far in the background on the left is Parsons Elementary School. This open field is now a subdivision of homes. (Courtesy Linda Bromund.)

In the early 1960s, Larry Champion purchased a larger gas station from Warren Bourassa. It was across the street from his on North Gibraltar Road and Blakely Street. The station was bigger and had more bays to accommodate automobiles needing service. The station became known as Champs. The part of Champs gas station facing North Gibraltar Road in this photograph was originally the back of the station. The road actually curved around to the other side, which eventually became Wilson Street when North Gibraltar Road was straightened. (Courtesy Linda Bromund.)

First Congregational Church of Gibraltar activated a building committee on November 1, 1963. Ground was broken on August 8, 1965, and the church was completed in 1966. It is located on Bayview Drive.

Putting on the bell tower finished construction of the church, and on October 23, 1966, Rev. Harold Aldrin dedicated the present building. The church today also serves as a community food bank.

The First Baptist Church of Gibraltar conducted its first service on October 2, 1953, in the old Gibraltar School. At that first service, 23 persons were present. After the old school burned down in 1954, the congregation held its services in Parsons Elementary School until its current building was completed in 1955. Burton Huth was the pastor and also served as the Gibraltar Cub Scout leader.

Early in 1958, a Catholic Mission Church was organized in Gibraltar, and Sunday masses were held in the Parsons Elementary School auditorium. Church pews from St. Peter's Church in Detroit were stored in Ross Denison's barn in 1959. When the church was completed in 1961, the stored pews were cleaned up and installed. The dedication of the church and the first mass was held on December 2, 1961, with Cardinal John Dearden presiding.

Among the many architectural highlights in Gibraltar, the most prominent and visible is the water tower on Adams Drive. This structure was never a lighthouse, though many people up to the present day have thought so. Henry Chaney built the tower in the 1800s to obtain water for use in his house and barns and in case of fire. The water was pumped by a windmill from the Detroit River to the storage tank on top of the tower. Ice was stored on the first two floors within stone walls two feet thick. The original tower burned down and was rebuilt in 1906. This tower, still intact, is a private residence.

A retired freighter captain had the pilothouse taken from a dismantled ship. It was hauled through the canals and placed on Worth Street and converted into a house. Due to a fire around 1976, the home is no longer there.

Mystery has surrounded this home on Adams Drive. Mr. Chaney, a grandson of Edmund Hall, joined three houses into one and then built the surrounding walls to insure his privacy. Chaney, fearing that someone was out to get him, constructed a tunnel running from the house to the back barn for use in an emergency. He lived here during the 1920s and 1930s, before moving to Oregon to become a lumberman. The existence of the tunnel led to rumors that the building may have been part of the Underground Railroad, but this complex was not in existence at that time. The home was also never a convent, and the "Purple Gang" never lived there. The home still stands, but it is vacant.

Six

WILDLIFE CONSERVATION AND ARTISTS

There are many canals and back creeks to paddle through on a kayak or fishing boat. In the background of this photograph is the bridge over South Gibraltar Road. On the left is the Lake Erie Metropark. (Courtesy Fay Blakely Steelman.)

A good day's catch is displayed on this boat on Lake Erie in the early 1950s. Gibraltar is located where the Detroit River opens into Lake Erie. For all of the back canals and creeks, there is even more open water on the river and lake, which makes for great fishing and duck hunting. (Courtesy Fay Blakely Steelman.)

In the fall of 1950, duck hunters get ready for a trip. On the far right is Governor Williams. Hy Dahlka is standing next to him. (Courtesy Fred Wall.)

Clive Taylor, a lifelong resident of Gibraltar, is seen here standing in his punt boat with his dog Rascal. A punt boat is a flat-bottom, shallow boat used for hunting in marshes. Taylor is a nine-time grand champion of the Pointe Mouillee Duck Hunters Tournament. Pointe Mouillee is a state game area located just south of Gibraltar. (Courtesy Clive Taylor.)

Gibraltar is home to many wildlife artists and duck carvers. Here, well-known artist Jim Foote sits in front of one of his paintings and holds two of his carvings. Foote, a resident of Gibraltar for 27 years, passed away in 2004. At an early age, he began carving duck decoys and preferred to study nature. In his 40s, he became involved with professional bird carving and entered contests. He won many decoy competitions in the 1970s. In the late 1970s, he started to focus on painting wildlife scenes and the production of edition prints of his paintings. The original painting seen here hangs in the Gibraltar Department of Public Works. (Courtesy Fred Wall.)

Tom Shumate is standing in his yard on Horse Island, holding two of the decoys he carved. Shumate, a lifelong resident of Gibraltar, was the son of Charles Shumate, the town's first mayor, and high school principal Helen Shumate. He had a passion for art, and as a child always drew wildlife, ducks, and birds and couldn't wait until fall, when he could repaint his dad's decoys. Retirement gave him the time to pursue his hobby. Inspired daily by his waterfront views, he continued to carve and paint waterfowl and birds, work that brought him acclaim. Tom's son Craig is also an avid wildlife artist. (Courtesy Bob Tomasik.)

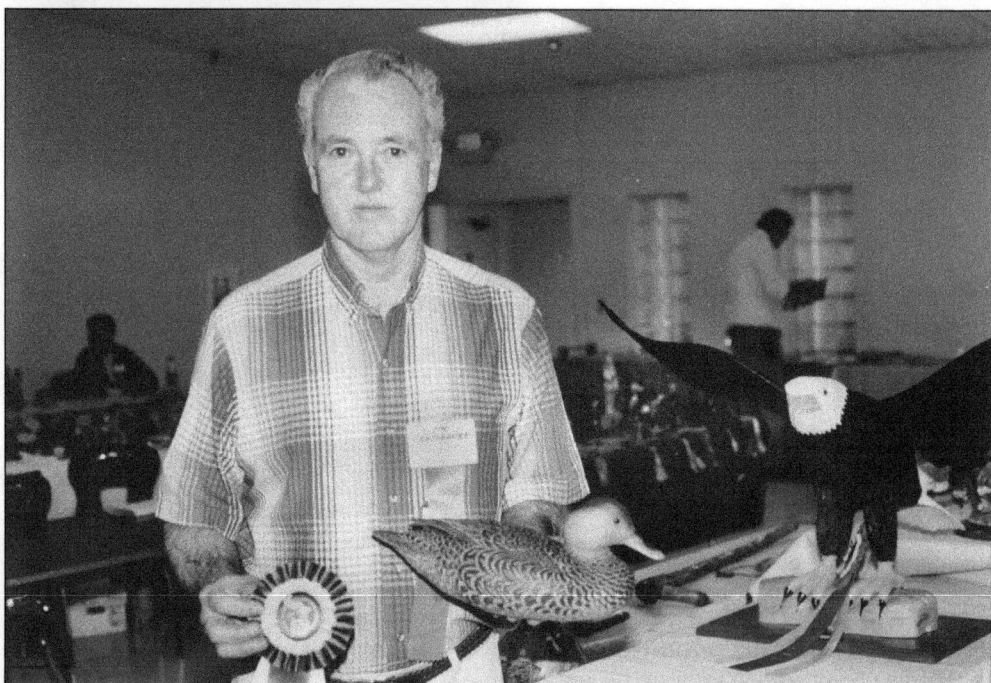

Jim Canterbury holds a blue ribbon and one of his prize-winning carvings. This decorative pintail hen decoy won first best of show. Jim is a longtime resident of Gibraltar. As well as being a prize-winning carver, he is also a painter. (Courtesy Jim Canterbury.)

Hunting, fishing, and trapping have always been mainstays in this area for providing food and for making a living. Muskrats have long been trapped for their fur and for food. Catholics are able to eat muskrat on Friday during Lent, because the muskrat is considered equivalent to a fish, since it lives in water. Clive Taylor (left), Fred Wall (center), and Chuck LeFleur are shown cooking muskrat dinners in their Lake Erie Lobster T-shirts. The Gibraltar Rotary has been sponsoring these dinners for years, and the event always sells out.

In the late 1950s, the McLouth Steel Corporation was looking to expand its operations on the water for blast furnaces as well as to be able to bring freighters in and out. The proposed site is the area seen here squared off, extending into the Detroit River. This area is the Humbug Marsh. The project was never carried out. (Courtesy Robert Wright.)

This is a current aerial photograph of the Humbug Marsh (upper center). The Steel Rolling Holdings Company (formerly McLouth Steel) is behind it. The island shown in the Detroit River is Humbug Island. On the far left is the city of Gibraltar, with the docks of Humbug Marina jutting out into the Detroit River. The squared-off sections on the right side of the photograph are in neighboring Trenton. Gibraltar has always been a natural wetland area. Over time, the dredging of creeks to form the canals and islands left only the Humbug Marsh as the last mile of natural shoreline on the Detroit River. The US Fish and Wildlife Service acquired this land in 2004. Today, it is the International Wildlife Refuge, a protected area. (Courtesy Michigan SeaGrant.)

EPILOGUE

After McLouth Steel closed its doors in 1993, some local businesses closed their doors as well. Because of increased gas prices, lack of jobs, and heightened security at the borders, the boating industry is not what it once was either.

However, as our history shows, when once-thriving businesses, such as the shipbuilding industry, come to an end, others takes their place, such as the McLouth Steel Corporation. To quote Gibraltar's first village president, Hy Dahlka, "When zoning was first done, we realized what we had and instead of thinking that we were ever going to have a big retail business in town as neighboring towns might, we knew that we never would because we are off the beaten path, we are on a spur here off the main road, but we have something other communities did not have and that is water. That makes us unique." If residents follow this thought and try not to make Gibraltar something that it is not, the city will rebound. Throughout the history of Gibraltar, its strong-willed residents have made it through the worst of times.

Gibraltar has come back to the beginning. Larger cities have used up all of their space and are now looking for green spaces for parks and gardening. Here in Gibraltar, hunting and fishing are still abundant. Wildlife such as the bald eagle has come back. Gibraltar is still wooded and surrounded by green space, bordered by the International Wildlife Refuge on the north, which is the Humbug Marsh, and the Lake Erie Metropark on the south. Studies show that green space attracts businesses, creates jobs, and raises property values. Today, the population of Gibraltar is 4,656. It is still a great little city—just ask anyone who lives here—and will one day be, yet again, on the way to revitalization.

The Gibraltar Historical Museum was founded in 2008 and reopened on May 6, 2012, with new hours and a new format. The museum is documenting the history of Gibraltar for future generations and welcomes visitors the first Sunday of every month from 2:00 p.m. to 4:00 p.m. Patrons may also reach the museum by calling the Gibraltar City Hall at 734-676-3900 or emailing gibraltarhm@yahoo.com.

Visit us at
arcadiapublishing.com

www.ingramcontent.com/pod-product-compliance
Lightning Source LLC
Chambersburg PA
CBHW050625110426
42813CB00007B/1722